T5-AFQ-987

CRISISPOINTS FOR WOMEN

WHEN YOU CAN'T GET ALONG

GLORIA CHISHOLM

NAVPRESS

A MINISTRY OF THE NAVIGATORS
P.O. BOX 6000, COLORADO SPRINGS, COLORADO 80934

The Navigators is an international Christian organization. Jesus Christ gave His followers the Great Commission to go and make disciples (Matthew 28:19). The aim of The Navigators is to help fulfill that commission by multiplying laborers for Christ in every nation.

NavPress is the publishing ministry of The Navigators. NavPress publications are tools to help Christians grow. Although publications alone cannot make disciples or change lives, they can help believers learn biblical discipleship, and apply what they learn to their lives and ministries.

© 1990 by Gloria Chisholm
All rights reserved, including translation
ISBN 08910-93311

Cover illustration by Earl Keleny.

CRISISPOINTS FOR WOMEN series edited by
Judith Couchman.

This series offers God's hope and healing for life's challenges.

All Scripture quotations in this publication are from the *Holy Bible: New International Version* (NIV). Copyright © 1973, 1978, 1984, International Bible Society. Used by permission of Zondervan Bible Publishers.

Printed in the United States of America

C O N T E N T S

To my kids, my friends, my enemies,
for the many opportunities
to engage in conflict and to grow.

ACKNOWLEDGMENTS

I want to thank Martha Erickson and Mary Ann Green, women I've never met in person, who faithfully encouraged and prayed for me as I wrote this Bible study.

I also want to thank Judith Couchman and NavPress for the opportunity to write about *conflict*—not my favorite pastime, but an activity with which I'm all too familiar. ∎

You Can Do It

*Begin to confront your
relationship conflicts.*

*A number of years ago, a man in New
York made the mistake of drinking
some clam chowder that was so hot it
burned his esophagus, doing perma-
nent damage that made it impossible
for him to swallow. The only solution
his doctors could devise was to pull
out a portion of his stomach lining so
that he could put food directly into his
stomach.*

*It does not sound like a very tasty
way to eat, but one side benefit was
that his doctors had the opportunity of
observing how his emotions affected his
digestion.*

*One fact quickly became apparent.
Nothing was more stressful than his relationship with people. Anger, resentment,
or bitterness would raise the acid level*

7

abruptly and cause his stomach lining to swell.

As they watched, his stomach told the story of a friendship gone astray. The stomach wall turned red, began to bleed, and developed an ulcer. In other words, that churning feeling in your stomach when a friendship goes astray is not just a feeling. Bad friendships destroy good stomachs![1]

What causes a relationship to break? Or when you stay together, but tension hinders you from acting natural around each other? Or when everything you say to each other turns sour?

It's called conflict. A clash of interests, personalities, opinions, lifestyles, or other things that erect a barrier between you and somebody. Worse yet, your individual approaches to disagreement can be so different that reaching a resolution looks hopeless.

HOPE FOR RESOLUTION

So when conflict rages on, is there hope for resolution? Absolutely.

This study guide explains how to involve God in the conflict so you can move through it and emerge as a winner. Not as a winner who always gets her way. But as someone who's defeated the enemy of her soul (who wants to destroy relationships) and the selfish drive to prove someone wrong so she can always be right.

Alone or in group study, this guide will help you discover creative methods of resolving conflict. You'll read about others like yourself who made the courageous decision to confront conflicts, even though they risked pain and rejection. And you'll learn to recognize different kinds of conflict and to choose your responses.

You can use this study guide in many ways. The introductory article and five Bible lessons will assist you in:

- Support or discussion groups.

- Scriptural support for counseling others.

- Personal growth and meditative reflection.

- One-on-one interaction or friendship development.

- Introducing women to a personal God who cares about them.

While this study will guide you through relationship problems, it's not an instant cure-all or ultimate answer book. It's meant to point you to the one true source of love and conflict resolution—Jesus Christ. ∎

—GLORIA CHISHOLM

NOTE
1. Gary Inrig, *Quality Friendship* (Chicago, IL: Moody Press, 1981), page 97.

The Only Way Out Is Through It

*Lasting relationships require
healthy conflicts.*

> *It was a mid-life reevaluation. I started
> to reevaluate my relationships with men,
> my relationship with the church, with my
> family . . . everything.*
>
> *All my coping mechanisms, all my
> values, everything that my family and
> society had given me, disintegrated. They
> didn't work. They left me with confusion,
> doubt, and conflict in every area of my
> life: conflicts religiously, conflicts as a
> mother, conflicts as a wife, conflicts as an
> in-law, conflicts as a daughter.*[1]

At thirty-nine years old, Phyllis suddenly
found herself in conflict with everything and
everyone most important to her. She was a
college graduate, teacher, mother, divorcee,
and minister. And the crisis was so big, it
took over ten years to resolve it.

Like Phyllis, I experienced my own mid-life reevaluation a few years back. I questioned every value and principle upon which I'd built my life. The tremor affected my relationships, both with God and people.

Up until that point, I'd managed relationships fairly well. Like many women, I'd surrounded myself with people who agreed with me on the important issues—or at least what I thought were the important issues. Life moved along nicely. No one sensed the internal rumblings that would crack my belief system and shake all of my relationships. Not even me.

Then one day it burst out. I suddenly found myself asking, "Why are we doing this?" It was as if my mind had formed into a big question mark. I questioned every routine in every structure of my life: church, family, relationships.

My devotional times grew irregular, and God and I spent much time engaged in conflict.

"But why, God? How? What for?"

It shocked me. It was all new to me. I'd experienced minor disagreements in relationships before: fender-benders. But I didn't like—or know how to handle—the fiery crashes occurring now. Yet I couldn't seem to keep the collisions from happening. Walking in integrity suddenly demanded that I ask tough questions.

The integrity part was okay. But I hadn't counted on the aftermath—the effects the crisis had on my relationships. That's when I learned—the hard way—that conflict can be either destructive or productive, depending on each individual's commitment to personal growth.

DESTRUCTIVE VS. PRODUCTIVE

In the book of Acts, the New Testament church brims with stories of conflict—between person and person and between people and their God. Not all of the conflicts proved productive. Peter and John conflicted with the Sadducees and landed in jail (4:1-3). Ananias and Sapphira conflicted with God and Peter—and died for it (5:1-10). Paul and Barnabas "sharply disagreed and parted company" (15:39).

So as believers, why does conflict surprise us? After all, we're still humans. And humans differ widely on politics, religion, philosophy, lifestyle—you name it. Often we don't really mean to, but we attack and hurt each other. We must remember we're sinners saved by grace—not to perfection.

Of course, God works in our hearts, making us more like Him. We can't overlook His power and principles to excuse our sin. But neither can we minimize the human element in conflict. It always seems ready to jump forward and mess up things when God wants to produce His life in a situation.

At times, we echo Charlie Brown's dog,

Snoopy, who cries, "There's no one who causes more trouble in this world than humans. They drive me crazy. I get so mad when I think about humans that I could scream!"[2]

But being human—and the inevitable nature of conflict—doesn't excuse us from replacing destructive conflicts with productive ones. Romans 12:21 admonishes us, "Do not be overcome by evil, but overcome evil with good."

So how do we discern the difference between destructive and productive conflict? It's a simple cause-and-effect relationship. Destructive conflict tears people and relationships apart. Productive conflict motivates growth in individuals and knits them together more closely than before.

When ideas, views, or personalities clash, we can choose to move in either a destructive or productive direction. Even when the other person is out of control and wants destruction, we can choose our response to conflict. Determined by our response, the conflict can produce positive growth in us, no matter what direction the other person chooses.

It's important to remember that God uses conflict for our good—when we let Him. Since God values relationships, He wants them to unite us into a body of believers that brings Him glory. With that in mind, take a look at these options for responding to conflict, both negative and positive.

"You don't even care!" I faced my friend squarely. "This thing you're doing happens to be hurting me."

Cary shook her head. "I'm sorry, but it's your problem. You're asking me to change for you. But I am who I am. If who I am hurts you, then I don't know what to say."

Was I asking too much of Cary? Was I making unfair demands? Did I need to just accept her? I didn't know if I could do that. I knew one thing: I couldn't now. I hurt. And because of my disapproval and unrealistic expectations, she hurt, too.

We parted.

We were both Christians and loved God deeply. But in our humanity, Cary and I had failed miserably at loving each other. Since the conflict started several months before, both of us had experienced a chain of reactions.

We didn't realize it at the time, but our reactions were common to people in conflict. Because of our sinful natures, we reacted to conflict with self-protective actions and emotions.

Denying the conflict. Just like people who grieve a tragedy or death, our first response to conflict can be denial. Consciously or subconsciously, we deny that the conflict exists.

We move into denial for various reasons: to avoid confrontation; to hope the conflict will go away; to bolster a belief that Christians shouldn't fight; to avoid revealing our imperfections; to minimize stress. All of these motivations result in the same action: ignoring the problem—and the possibility that it could get worse from our inattention.

For example, a woman's husband is coming home later and later every night.

"Had to work late again," he announces as he enters the house.

She remembers driving past his office an hour before, looking for his car. It wasn't there. *He probably went out for a hamburger,* she tells herself.

The man kisses his wife, and the smell of alcohol gags her. She says nothing. If there's a conflict, she's afraid of what she may find out, of what she'll be forced to face.

But ignoring the problem won't suppress the eventual conflict. And the need for denial reveals that a conflict has already begun.

Escape from discomfort. Conflict threatens our comfort zones, our safety. The red flag goes up, the alarm blares. The neon sign flashes "Alert! Danger!" We might get hurt. So to avoid the discomfort, we run away.

The Bible cites many examples of those who, when facing conflict, decided to take off. Jesus' disciples accompanied Him to the Garden of Gethsemane to watch and pray. They kept falling asleep, but they probably woke up quickly when Judas arrived with "a large crowd armed with swords and clubs" (Matthew 26:47). A confrontation

16

erupted, and by the end of it, "all the disciples deserted him and fled" in fear (verse 56).

Adam and Eve (Genesis 3:8), Moses (Exodus 2:15), David (1 Samuel 21:10), Elijah (1 Kings 19:3), and Peter (Mark 14:68) also tried to avoid conflict. And some of these ran from confrontation more than once. They were definitely human.

Escape can take on emotional forms as well as physical ones. We run by escaping to the refrigerator, the telephone, the television, or inside ourselves to shut out confrontation.

Anger based on fear. Bonnie, the mother of a daughter born with spina bifida, erupted in anger at her husband when she really needed his comfort. Their daughter Laurie was in the hospital, getting ready for surgery. Bonnie explains:

> *I went to pick up Todd. . . . But when I got home, he wasn't there. . . . By the time we finally got hooked up and back to the hospital, they had taken Laurie into surgery. All I could think was,* What if she dies during this operation?
>
> *I really laid into Todd—right there in the hospital corridor, with people listening to us. And while I was doing it, I was wondering,* Why am I doing this? She's his daughter, too—he loves her as much as I do. He feels horrible that he missed seeing her before surgery. But . . . *I couldn't stop myself, the emotions were so strong.[3]*

17

Bonnie's violent anger was motivated by the fear that her daughter might die during surgery—that she might never see Laurie again. Fear caused Bonnie to blame Todd because she potentially faced a terrible loss she didn't want to confront.

Other times, anger wells from insecurities we don't want to face and fight. Author and teacher Jamie Buckingham tells us, "The cause of anger is not hate. The basic cause of anger is fear. Our anger is a facade we raise to hide our insecurities."[4] We're afraid of what conflict may expose about our broken selves.

Protective peacemaking. At the first sign of discord, people pleasers will immediately try to calm the rumblings. We won't even give conflict a chance to take hold. We say all the right things, the nice things, the things we hope will circumvent the problem. But we're really just capping the problem so tightly that someday it will explode.

People pleasers need the approval of others to feel secure. Conflict is extremely threatening to them because it requires honesty. And honesty often evokes displeasure from others. Our peacemaking efforts appear noble—even spiritual—but underneath we're protecting ourselves from pain.

Instant forgiveness. If peacemaking malfunctions and a conflict occurs, we often progress to instant forgiveness. Like peacemaking, instant forgiveness appears godly and noble. Doesn't the Bible tell us to forgive when offended (Mark 11:25)?

Yes, the principle is true. But again, it's a matter of motive. Are we forgiving because we truly, from our hearts, want to love one another? Or are we forgiving quickly to avoid a nasty fight, a messy conflict where we might suffer pain and rejection?

Forgiveness must always be a part of resolving conflict. But when we forgive to avoid conflict, we enable others to sin against us. Their resentment festers deep inside, unable to dissolve, because we've buried the conflict too quickly. We never dig to the root of the conflict and yank it out.

In reality, we've granted a pseudo-forgiveness. Later we find the conflict growing again. It wasn't resolved; it was just submerged.

GODLY RESPONSES

In her book *How to Say Goodbye,* Joanne Smith tells of a time when her husband Duane loaned a man in their church $5,000 to be paid back in full after ninety days.

Ninety days passed and the man began to avoid Duane, refusing phone calls and making himself scarce at church.

Duane's congenial personality soon began to change. He became angry and, eventually, turned bitter. When Joanne confronted him about it, Duane promised to take care of his attitude. Duane then called a meeting with the man, tore the contract to shreds, and forgave the debt. After that, Duane was free to be himself again.[5]

Our conflicts and resolutions may not be as dramatic as Duane's, but they still need careful attention.

So how do we practice godly responses to collisions with people? We must realize that conflict resolution is a process. As with any process, it involves several steps—and a lot of time.

Acknowledging sin. James exhorts, "Therefore, confess your sins to each other and pray for each other so that you may be healed" (James 5:16). Acknowledging our sin in the conflict is the first step toward resolution. Our confession enables other people to acknowledge their sin and opens the opportunity for prayer and healing.

Of course, our acknowledgment of sin does not mean other people will automatically do the same, but we have done the loving thing by being honest and humble. If no one else acknowledges anything, we've taken a step toward our own healing.

Holding steady. Since conflict usually takes time to work itself out, a waiting period is crucial to resolution. If they've emotionally closed themselves off, people have feelings to work through and release. They need time to open up to each other and to God so He can fulfill His purpose in their lives.

Scripture tells us, "Be still before the LORD and wait patiently for him" (Psalm 37:7). God's timing is perfect—that includes the right timing for conflict resolution. However, it's important to check our motives to make sure we're not "holding steady" just to avoid the conflict.

Choosing courage. Unless we're motivated by extreme anger, we often lack courage to confront the issues that cause our conflicts. We're too afraid. But Walter Anderson, editor of *Parade Magazine,* says, "Courage . . . is always and only one thing: It is acting *with* fear, not without it. To be brave, we must be afraid."[6]

I remember the time I confronted an authority figure who'd dealt with me dishonestly. "Okay, God, I'm scared to death," I prayed moments before the confrontation. "You're on."

Fear thrusts us on God's power and mercy. Acknowledging my fear helped me to choose courage. I didn't emerge from the conflict without wounds. But I've learned that victory is not determined by the absence of scars, but by our ability to step back and let God direct us.

So when we fear conflict, we can view it as an opportunity to let the Holy Spirit implant and develop God's courage in us (2 Chronicles 32:7-8).

Sacrificing our rights. Much conflict erupts out of the need to be right. It intensifies when people are so sure of their "rightness" that proving others wrong becomes their goal.

But if we follow Christ's example, we'll need to replace our need to be right with personal sacrifice. Jesus was "right" in that He deserved respect, worship, honor, and exaltation. He didn't deserve to die on a cross. But He sacrificed His rightness for our wrongness, our sin.

There's also a wrong kind of sacrificing. Modern-day martyrs, in their need to look good, will sacrifice themselves to make others feel sorry for or approve of them. But genuine self-sacrifice is motivated by love for others (Philippians 2:3-4).

Taking responsibility. When conflict arises, attacks begin. We get so busy defending ourselves, we often neglect our part in the conflict. We can too easily focus on other people's sins, blaming them for the turmoil and taking ourselves off the hook.

For example, if we're victims of abuse, we're tempted to blame that abusive conflict for all of our problems. While the abuser did perpetrate horrible crimes against us, we must also take responsibility for our part: allowing ourselves to be intimidated or victimized; hanging on to bitterness; refusing to be healed. Taking responsibility opens the doors to our healing.

To take responsibility is to humble ourselves before God (1 Peter 5:6) and to repent of our wrongdoings in the conflict (2 Corinthians 7:10). If other people are as anxious as we are to resolve the problem, our action will enable them to take responsibility, too. We've set an atmosphere for restoration.

Forgiving others. It's easy to discuss forgiveness as a godly principle; it's difficult to implement it in active conflict. Especially when we've been truly wronged, and the wrongdoers aren't sorry or repentant.

But forgiveness is crucial if we want to emerge from the conflict intact, without judgments and bitterness (Ephesians 4:32). Sometimes we'll need to forgive people face to face, sometimes, by ourselves before God.

One-shot forgiveness is possible, but more often, it's a process. We'll probably need to let go of anger, judgments, and hurt again and again and again . . . until we're free.

TRUST AND HOPE

The Bible says love "always trusts" (1 Corinthians 13:7). So throughout conflict, we must practice an ongoing trust in God to bring good and growth out of the situation. He is for us in our conflicts. But as hard as it is to understand, He's also for the people with whom we've locked horns. As much as we'll let Him, He is working to accomplish maximum growth for us as individuals and for our relationships.

Trusting God is the key that unlocks our conflicts and sets us free to grow in Christlikeness. And isn't that the goal in our relationships, to be Jesus to each other?

To be Jesus to each other is to trust His involvement in our relationships. If we can do that, there's always hope for conflict resolution. ■

NOTES
  1. Alice Slaikeu Lawhead, *The Lie of the Good Life* (Portland, OR: Multnomah Press, 1989), page 140.

2. Robert L. Short, *The Parables of Peanuts* (New York, Evanston, and London: Harper & Row, Publishers, 1968), page 47.
3. Lawhead, page 192.
4. Jamie Buckingham, *Where Eagles Soar* (Lincoln, VA: Chosen Books, 1980), page 169.
5. Joanne Smith and Judy Biggs, *How to Say Goodbye* (Lynnwood, WA: Aglow Publications, 1990), pages 78-80.
6. Walter Anderson, *The Greatest Risk of All* (Boston, MA: Houghton Mifflin Company, 1988), page 215.

Take an Honest Look

*Do you view conflict as positive
or negative?*

You can resolve your conflicts with others.
But before you begin, consider the following questions. If you're studying with
a group, you can still keep your answers
confidential.

The purpose: to find out where you
need the most help so God can give you
direction.

1. Why do you want to resolve conflict in
   your relationships?

2. What are your greatest weaknesses that contribute to conflicts?

3. Use the following graph to measure the level of tension in your primary relationships. For each person, circle the number that represents the tension in that relationship. Scale: "1" = no tension; "10" = extreme tension.

	LITTLE OR NO TENSION							EXTREME TENSION		
Husband	1	2	3	4	5	6	7	8	9	10
Child	1	2	3	4	5	6	7	8	9	10
Parent	1	2	3	4	5	6	7	8	9	10
Relative	1	2	3	4	5	6	7	8	9	10
Friend	1	2	3	4	5	6	7	8	9	10
Boss	1	2	3	4	5	6	7	8	9	10

4. What causes tension in the relationships that rated high in conflict?

5. Consider the relationship in which you're experiencing the most conflict. If a friend came to you with the same problem, how would you counsel and pray for her? Why is it difficult to do the same for yourself?

6. In this difficult relationship, picture an imaginary scene in which both of you confront gut issues. Write a scenario that plays out your worst fears. Then write another scene that reflects your hope for resolution.

7. Read Romans 12:18. What's a first step you can take toward living at peace with the people you're in conflict with?

8. Write a prayer to God that expresses your need for His help in resolving conflict. ■

When Conflicting Personalities Conflict

*Is it a destructive
or productive clash?*

Gayle clutched the receiver. "What do you mean, I need to relax? Those invitations should have gone out a week ago!"

"Maybe so," Alice conceded. "But you're lucky you have any help at all. This is a bad time of year to throw a goodbye party with everyone on vacation and. . . ." Alice's voice droned on.

Gayle had thought everyone would be grateful to her for planning their friend Carol's goodbye party. Instead, they were complaining about Gayle's bossiness.

Hurt, both women hung up.

DEALING WITH FEELINGS

Conflict. It happens to all of us. Our ages, our differences, our stress levels, our personalities all contribute to conflicts with others.

Whether it's a volatile eruption or an under-the-surface tension, conflicts surface everybody's feelings. So to handle conflict in a healthy and godly way, it's important to acknowledge your feelings.

1. How do you usually react during a conflict? List emotions as well as actions. Why do you respond this way?

REACTION	REASON

2. Read Romans 14:12-13. Why is it important to admit and "own" your feelings in a conflict?

3. What do the following verses tell you about godly responses during conflict?

Psalm 88:8-9

Proverbs 3:29-30

2 Corinthians 7:9-10

Ephesians 4:26-27

Colossians 3:8-10

4. How can these verses apply to your answers in question 1?

DESTRUCTIVE OR PRODUCTIVE

When you admit your feelings and understand how God wants you to respond, you can choose between destructive and productive conflict.

5. Based on the opening article to this study guide, describe the difference between destructive and productive conflict. Which type of conflict have you been involved in the most?

6. Do you think all conflict is negative or sinful? Explain.

7. a. Read the following Bible passages. In each conflict, identify the participants' responses. Then decide if these responses contributed to destructive (D) or productive (P) conflict. Place the appropriate letter beside each situation.

PEOPLE	RESPONSES
Saul and David (1 Samuel 18:1–19:1, 2 Samuel 1)	

PEOPLE	RESPONSES
Mordecai and Haman (Esther 3–4)	
Jesus and Peter (John 13:1,5-10)	

b. Can you see yourself in any of these examples? Explain.

8. When you choose to move conflict in a productive and godly direction, you will encounter opposition from Satan, the enemy. According to these verses, how does he work against you?

Acts 5:3

2 Corinthians 11:14-15

Ephesians 6:11-12

James 3:14-16

1 John 3:8

9. How does the Bible say you can resist Satan?

Ephesians 6:13-18

2 Timothy 3:12-17

James 4:7-10

10. Describe a strategy to defeat Satan the next time he tempts you toward destructive conflict.

11. Satan isn't the only culprit in conflict. Read James 1:13-15. How else are we tempted to engage in destructive conflict?

12. a. What personal weaknesses or sins most often move your relational conflicts in a destructive direction?

    b. How can you cooperate with God to change these?

13. Think of a recent or current conflict of yours. How does God want you to move this conflict in a productive direction? How can He help you? What is your part?

WHAT TO DO	GOD'S PART	MY PART
Galatians 5:13-26		
James 3:17-18		

This week, keep a log of relational conflicts. Observe these conflicts wherever you encounter them—in books, at work, in your home, at the movies, on television.

Mentally replay each conflict, and record the (1) participants, (2) reason(s) for the conflict, and (3) root causes. Then ask yourself,

- Were these destructive or productive conflicts?

- Were there similarities among the conflicts that caused them to be destructive or productive?

- How could the destructive conflicts have been turned into productive ones? Rewrite the conflict(s) to reflect these changes.

- What can these situations teach you about conflict? ∎

When You Want to Run

*How to hold steady if you
feel afraid.*

Beth sat rigid in the chair, gripping the armrests, as her boss outlined the terms and pay scale of her job adjustment.

No way, she thought. After ten years of faithful commitment to this company, she couldn't accept these terms and maintain her dignity.

Beth fought the impulse to get up and walk out the door.

REAL ISSUES

The desire to run from conflict is normal. We're afraid of getting battered in the clash. We're afraid to face the death of a relationship. We're afraid of pain and rejection. Worse yet, we're afraid of fear.

At this point, it's easy to avoid conflict. We can take one of three dishonest routes:

- Withdraw and continue without the person.

- Stay in the person's life, but refuse to share personally.

- Relate to the person with anger and sarcasm, avoiding the real issues.

1. Think of a conflict you're engaged in now. (If you don't have a current conflict, refer to a past encounter to complete this lesson.) What are the real issues—the root causes and struggles underneath the conflict?

2. What are you afraid of in this conflict?

3. Have you taken any of the three dishonest routes described earlier? Explain.

POTENTIAL LOSSES

In his challenging book *The Greatest Risk of All,* Walter Anderson identifies three types of losses that accompany risk. They are:

- **The positive loss:** the acknowledgment that what we have isn't enough.

- **The practical loss:** what we give up to move ahead.

- **The potential loss:** the tangible thing we lose if the risk does not work out.[1]

4. Confronting conflict is always a risk. Use the following chart to identify your possible losses in a current conflict. You may have more than one item in a category.

CONFLICT LOSSES	PRACTICAL LOSSES	POTENTIAL LOSSES

5. What losses are you most afraid of in this conflict? Why?

6. How probable is it that you'll experience these losses? Explain.

7. According to these verses, what happens to people who let fear control them?

Deuteronomy 20:1-4,8

Judges 7:2-3

GOD'S PROMISES

Instead of giving in to fear, God wants you to hold steady. To relax. To wait. To trust Him.

8. When conflict hits, what does Scripture tell us to do with fear? What does God promise you in the presence of fear?

COMMAND	PROMISE
Isaiah 8:12-13	Leviticus 26:6
Matthew 10:28	Psalm 34:4

COMMAND	PROMISE
Mark 5:36	Psalm 118:6
John 14:1	Romans 8:15
1 Peter 3:13-15	2 Timothy 1:7

HOLDING STEADY

When fear tempts us to run, it's time to hold steady, even when it looks like nothing's changing—or that the conflict's getting worse. During these times, it's most crucial to persevere, because sometimes it's rockiest right before a conflict resolution.

9. Think of the fears you face in a conflict you're involved in now. List one or more steps you can take to hold steady rather than run away from this conflict.

10. What are your expectations for the outcome of this conflict? Mark whether each expectation is realistic (R) or unrealistic (U).

11. Do unrealistic expectations keep you from holding steady? Do they make you give up? Explain.

12. What does God promise if you persevere?

2 Thessalonians 1:4-7

James 1:12

James 5:11

TAKING ACTION

13. Holding steady doesn't mean being inactive. List five positive actions you can take while you're holding steady. Also list negative actions that would hinder your progress toward conflict resolution.

POSITIVE	NEGATIVE

STOP RUNNING

This week, read Hebrews 11. Note the actions these biblical characters took by faith—without receiving the tangible fulfillment of God's promise (verse 39).

Write a commitment statement of how you will tackle conflict by faith, even if nothing tangible ever happens to resolve the situation. Start with, "By faith, I will. . . ." Then write what action you will take to conquer fear and to hold steady. ■

NOTE
  1. Walter Anderson, *The Greatest Risk of All* (Boston, MA: Houghton Mifflin Company, 1988), pages 37-38.

Loving Anyway

*Keeping your heart right through
the pain.*

The harsh words spilled out before Paula or
Joan could catch them. They hung in the air
with an intensity that caused both women to
back off from the conflict—and each other.

Later, Paula told a friend, "I don't
know when a friend has ever hurt me this
badly before. I feel betrayed, ripped open,
by Joan. I can't stand it. This hurts too
much."

Joan felt the same way about Paula.
"Every day, the pain of Paula's words stabs
me," she sobbed. "How can I resolve this conflict when I still feel so wounded?"

PURPOSE IN PAIN

Pain often accompanies conflict. If it's not
confronted, pain locks up our emotions, closes
us off from others, turns us into phonies, and

robs us of loving relationships.

Confronting pain isn't easy. We have to hurt in order to examine and to heal it. Yet Jesus stands as the example of One who confronted pain to administer healing. He died on the cross. He chose to hurt for us, keeping His focus on "the joy set before him" (Hebrews 12:2), so that we could be set free from sin.

1. God can use the pain in our lives. How do these verses apply to pain from conflict?

   Romans 8:17-18

   1 Peter 4:12-13

   1 Peter 5:10

2. Identify the relationship in which you suffer the most conflict. Describe the pain this relationship inflicts on you. Then, according to the verses in question 1, express how God may want to use this pain in your life.

3. Are God's purposes enough to motivate you to face the pain in this relationship? Be honest and explain.

ADMITTING TO FAULT

To deal honestly with pain, we must acknowledge the hurts we've inflicted on others. This includes the pain we've caused during the conflict or afterward when we shut ourselves off to a resolution.

4. Take another look at your most painful relationship. Consider the pain the other person experiences as a result of your conflict. Describe it below.

Sometimes a conflict arises and nobody's at fault. Two people just disagree without harm to each other. Other times, both parties are guilty of sinning and inflicting pain.

5. Think again about your painful relationship. On the barometers below, indicate your honest feelings about how much you're contributing to the conflict. Fill in the bars when "0" = you're not responsible and "10" = you're totally responsible.

	0 1 2 3 4 5 6 7 8 9 10
Am I at fault?	
Am I causing my pain?	
Am I causing his/her pain?	

The purpose of this exercise is *not to place blame on the other person.* Rather, it's to help you decipher *your negative contribution* to the conflict—to face the pain of your own wrongdoings.

6. How have you contributed to the destructive force of this conflict? List specific words and actions. What sins have you committed during this conflict?

GOD'S EXPECTATIONS

7. What are God's expectations concerning your fault and sins in this conflict?

Matthew 5:21-25

Matthew 5:29-30

James 5:16

1 John 1:9

8. Based on these verses, plan what you must do to confess your part in this conflict. Are you willing to take these actions? Explain, including when.

9. Read Matthew 5:38-42. Aside from confessing your sins, how does God want you to treat the person you're in conflict with?

In each phase of a conflict, we can choose to stay open and to love the person who's opposing us, even if we've been hurt. If we count the cost, we can make an intelligent choice to love, knowing what we may suffer in return (see Luke 14:25-33).

To love during conflict is to "lay down our lives" as Christ did for us (1 John 3:16). It is to push past the pain and to make a self-sacrificing choice. It is to give up our rights so that we can keep our hearts open.

The good news is that loving others can help heal the hurt in our own hearts—if we continue to involve God in the process.

10. What must you give up to love through this conflict?

    1 Corinthians 13:11

    Ephesians 4:29-31

Philippians 3:13

Colossians 3:8-9

11. Practically speaking, how can you show
    your love?

Romans 15:7

Ephesians 4:15,32

Colossians 3:12

LOVING ANYWAY

12. What are loving actions and attitudes
    you can express toward the person who's
    causing you pain? If the conflict includes
    serious abuse by this person, ask God for
    wisdom about confronting sin and show-
    ing "tough love."

GETTING HONEST

This week, ask somebody close to you to honestly answer these questions:

- Have I ever hurt you?

- How have I hurt you?

- Was it an isolated incident, or do you see it as an ongoing pattern?

- How can God use me to heal the hurt?

- How can I love you better in the future?

Once you've collected the answers, pray about them, thanking God for revealing any failure to love well. Ask God for forgiveness and for His love in your current conflict and in future relationships. ■

Blocked!

*What to do when nobody wants
to budge.*

Rachel couldn't believe her ears. "What? You
don't really believe *that*?"

"I most certainly do," Kay shot back. "It's
what the Bible says."

"The Bible doesn't say that at all. It's
your interpretation."

"Right. And what you believe isn't *your*
interpretation, I suppose?"

"I guess we just disagree."

In the next few days, Kay and Rachel
tried to discuss the issue again. Tempers
flared and harsh words bounced back and
forth. They were blocked by conflict.

LOCKING IN

Confession and forgiveness can resolve the
most difficult of conflicts. As long as both
people are open to the Lord and to their

individual contributions to the conflict, there's always hope for resolution.

However, there's no guarantee that both people will cooperate. Too often, we lock into our positions and bury the issue—or write each other off as hopeless. We give up just short of a resolution.

1. Who is blocking the resolution of your current conflict? For each statement below, place the initials of the person(s) who express(es) this opinion. Not all statements will apply to your conflict. Add your own statements, too.

_____ "It's hopeless. He *always*. . . ." (Judgment)

_____ "I'm right. She's wrong." (Arrogance)

_____ "I'll never, ever forgive her." (Unforgiveness)

_____ "I don't care. I don't need them." (Self-protection)

_____ "I refuse to discuss it any further." (Stubbornness)

_____ "Oh, what's the point? I'm awful. They hate me." (Self-pity)

_____ "She doesn't know what's right like I do." (Self-righteousness)

_____ "I don't need any more stress right now." (Fear)

_____ Other:

_____ Other:

2. Are you and/or the other person committing sin by blocking this conflict? Are you employing any of the self-protective reactions explained in this booklet's opening article? In what ways?

3. Review question 2 in lesson 3. If you're blocking a resolution to this conflict, will you take biblical steps toward confession, forgiveness, and unlocking the conflict? Explain.

4. If you've taken these steps, but the other person won't budge or admit wrongdoing, what can you do? See Galatians 6:1-4.

5. What happens to people who don't acknowledge and confess their sins?

Psalm 66:18

Galatians 6:7-8

1 John 1:8

ANOTHER VIEWPOINT

6. When you are locked in a conflict that seems hopeless, what does the Bible promise?

2 Corinthians 1:10

2 Corinthians 2:14

Hebrews 6:18-20

2 Peter 1:3

While these verses promise God's help, they don't guarantee we'll get our own way. Victory in Christ doesn't mean a triumph of our own opinions. It means drawing on His strength to behave in a godly manner.

7. If you've done what you can, what negative choices could lock you further into the conflict? What positive choices could lead toward resolution?

POSITIVE	NEGATIVE

8. Think about your most difficult conflict. Are you willing to work toward conflict resolution, even if the person never agrees with your opinion? How could you begin to do this?

SETTING GOALS

We have both desires and goals for our relationships. We can *desire* specific movement in our interaction with others, but we can't set *goals* for their behavior.

Conflict happens when we set goals for other people. They resist our control of their lives. So the only goals we can set for blocked conflict are actions for ourselves.

9. List the goals you have for yourself in this difficult relationship. Then list the desires you have for the other person.

GOALS FOR ME	DESIRES FOR HIM/HER

10. How can you deal with the desire you have for the other person's behavior? How can you pursue your goals?

What if you've done and said all that you can do or say and no progress is made? What if one or both of you can't resolve your negative feelings and continue in the relationship?

11. Read Galatians 6:9-10. What can you do if negative feelings don't get resolved?

12. Should you ever give up on a locked conflict? A conflictive relationship? Explain.

13. Read James 4:8-17. How does this passage relate to losing a relationship because of conflict?

MOVING THE BLOCK

This week, pray about your relationship that's blocked in conflict. Make a list of goals for yourself and desires for the relationship. If the relationship is still amiable, present your list to the other person and talk about how to resolve the conflict.

If the relationship is not amiable, present your lists to God and commit to (1) repent any time you sin in this conflict, (2) actively love the other person whenever you have the opportunity, and (3) trust that God is moving in the other person's heart.

Then wait, and watch God move in the situation. With God as your partner, you can bring closure to conflict, no matter what choices the other person makes. ■

Bringing Closure to Conflict

*You can initiate healing
and resolution.*

Marta rounded a corner at the grocery
store and collided with another shopper's
cart.

"Oh, I'm sorry! I didn't meant to do that,"
she apologized while backing her cart out of
the aisle.

"Marta? It's me, Darlene," said the
other shopper. Marta looked up, and both
women smiled sheepishly. Then they talked
briefly and planned a lunch date for the
next week.

During lunch, the women set straight
a conflict they'd left unresolved a year
before. Time and distance had healed their
wounds.

At one point, Marta asked, "What was
the big deal back then, anyway?"

"I don't know," replied Darlene. "It all
seems so silly now."

Not all conflict resolves the same way. The Bible says not to let the sun set while we are still angry (Ephesians 4:26), and that's a command we should take seriously. But often it takes many sunsets before a conflict can be resolved. We need time to work out the issues.

So in order to bring closure to a conflict, we might take a combination of these paths:

- Immediate or timely resolution of the conflict.

- Resolution with the help of an objective third person.

- Resolution after time and distance have mellowed both of the conflicting people.

- Resolution inside a person when her opponent won't cooperate in a solution.

1. Consult the above list of resolutions and fill in the following chart as it relates to your current conflict.

   For each alternative, ask yourself, "What can I do if I choose this method of resolution? How would it affect the relationship?"

RESOLUTION	EFFECTS
Immediate or timely	
Third person	
Time and distance	
Inward only	

2. Try to envision an immediate or timely resolution to your current conflict where everyone wins. Write the climactic scene of action: each person gives a little and takes a little. Most important, everyone walks away feeling a sense of completion.

3. How realistic is this scenario for your current conflict? Can you do anything to bring it about? Explain.

4. What do you lose by not bringing a timely closure to this conflict? What do you gain?

LOSSES	GAINS

OBJECTIVE THIRD PERSON

5. What would be the advantages and disadvantages of asking an objective person to help resolve the conflict?

ADVANTAGES	DISADVANTAGES

6. To arbitrate your conflict, what qualities should this person possess? Who could fill this role for you?

TIME AND DISTANCE

7. How could time and distance help you reach conflict resolution at a later date?

8. a. What are the pitfalls of putting time and distance between you and your opponent?

b. How can you avoid these problems?

INWARD RESOLUTION

9. If you've done everything you can, and the person still refuses to budge, how can you resolve the conflict inside yourself? See Ephesians 4:31, Hebrews 12:14-15, and 2 Peter 1:5-9.

10. After you've resolved the conflict inwardly, what can you still do?

   Matthew 6:33-34

Philippians 4:4-9

Hebrews 4:14-16

CHOOSING CLOSURE

11. Which of the methods we've looked at would effectively bring closure to your conflict? Is your choice based on avoidance? Explain.

12. After you resolve this conflict, you must decide if you want to continue a relationship with this person.

    a. List the pros and cons of relating to this person in the future. What are your motives for each?

PROS AND MOTIVES	CONS AND MOTIVES

b. What do you feel God wants you to do about relating to this person in the future?

13. Whether or not a close relationship continues, how does God want you to regard the other person?

   Philippians 2:3-8

1 Thessalonians 4:11

1 Thessalonians 5:15

14. If the other person has rejected you, you will need time to grieve the relationship. Make a list of the things you will miss and let go of them, one by one.

15. Once you've reached closure, how can you keep from reviewing the conflict in your mind? What can you do if the conflict erupts between you again?

Ultimately, God is the one to trust for the
resolution of our conflicts. Because God
loves us, He is working everything out for
our good (Romans 8:28). We can trust Him
with the final results—as long as the good-
ness of His character is established deep
inside us.

16. Look at these biblical characters who
    chose to trust God. What did they risk?
    What did they gain?

RISK	GAIN
Job (Job 42:1-6,10-13)	
Mary (Luke 1:26-55)	

RISK	GAIN
Paralytic (Luke 5:18-25)	

17. a. What can you gain by trusting God
    with the future?

    b. Are you willing to risk trusting God?
    If so, how can you show that you
    trust Him?

Is it time for you to bring closure to a conflict? Which of these options do you need to initiate?

❏ Go to the other person and talk about the conflict.

❏ Work out a resolution with the person.

❏ Forgive each other. Or at least do your part to forgive.

❏ Release the person and your negative feelings.

❏ Determine how to relate to this person in the future.

❏ Grieve the loss of the relationship— and say goodbye.

If you haven't already, begin the process of closure this week. Ask God to help you to let go and commit the conflict to Him until your healing is complete. ■

Digging Deeper

*Additional passages for conflict
resolution.*

You will need to record your answers for this
section on additional sheets of paper.

LESSON ONE

1. Read Ephesians 5:17. From your experience, list three things that lead to foolish
   (destructive) conflict and three steps to
   discover God's will (productive conflict).

2. Isaiah 14:12-15 shows God and Satan
   engaged in conflict. What were Satan's
   sins? How do these same sins turn your
   conflicts in a destructive direction?

3. Christ stood on the edge of destructive
   conflict with His skeptics. Examine
   Matthew 19:1-12, John 4:5-26, and
   8:12-30. How did Jesus turn potential

destructive conflict in a productive direction? What were the results?

4. Study Proverbs 15:1. How can anger turn into destructive conflict? Find more proverbs that emphasize this truth.

LESSON TWO

1. What strategies do you employ to avoid conflict? How do those strategies keep you from social and spiritual growth?

2. To avoid conflict, Peter denied the Lord in Luke 22:54-62. How could he have handled the situation with integrity?

3. Read 2 Corinthians 3:4-6. How can you become competent in handling difficult people? List three ways you can appropriate God's competence when you need it.

LESSON THREE

1. Read Hebrews 12:15. How can you extend grace to those with whom you're in conflict? How can you avoid bitterness?

2. Read Genesis 4:3-16. Especially consider verses 6 and 7. What makes you so angry that you sin? How can you master your anger and choose to love?

3. See Philippians 1:9. How can "knowledge and depth of insight" make your love "abound more and more" in conflict?

4. Think of a time in your life when hatred stirred up dissension (Proverbs 10:12). How could love have covered all wrongs?

LESSON FOUR

1. Read Hebrews 12:1-4. How can you keep from growing weary and losing heart in a difficult conflict?

2. Matthew 5:43-44 says to pray for your enemies. What blocks you from doing this? What should you pray for? Can praying for your enemies ever become an excuse for not facing your sins? Explain.

3. Releasing your grasp helps to unlock conflict. In a current conflict, what is the most difficult thing to let go?

LESSON FIVE

1. Read Philippians 3:14. In thinking about conflict, what does it mean to "press on toward the goal to win the prize for which God has called" you?

2. Study 1 Peter 1:6-7. How can your faith be proved genuine through conflict? What are the results of a faith that is tested by conflict?

3. Examine Matthew 18:15-18. What is the biblical procedure for bringing closure to conflict? Is this a possibility or necessity in a current conflict of yours? Explain.

4. Find at least five assurances in Proverbs 16 that will assist you in bringing closure to conflict. How can you practically apply them to your current conflict?

Remember: Conflict resolution is a process, not a quick fix-up to avoid responsibility. ■

Getting Along Together

Questions for your small group.

THE ONLY WAY OUT IS THROUGH IT

1. Read Psalm 133 together. How does destructive conflict hinder unity? Have you ever experienced God's blessing as a result of uniting with someone? Explain.
2. In one-on-one conflict, what is your greatest fear? In group conflict? Could a support group help alleviate your fear?
3. When others deny conflict, what is the most loving thing you can do for them? What do you want others to do when you're in denial?
4. Do you usually blame yourself for conflict? Or do you usually blame others? What can you do to balance the responsibility when engaged in conflict?
5. Peacemaking and forgiveness can become strategies for avoiding conflict. How can

you recognize when this happens?
6. What does it mean to be confrontable?
   How can you develop that attitude?
7. Examine Proverbs 3:5-6. Why can it be
   more difficult to trust God during conflicts than at other times?

LESSON ONE

1. Choose two people in your group and fab-
   ricate an issue on which they disagree.
   Ask the group to choose sides, discuss
   the issue, and negotiate a resolution.
   Then discuss productive and destructive
   aspects of the conflict.
2. What are the warning signs of a productive conflict turning into a destructive one? What can you do when this
   happens?
3. Read Psalm 142:3. Where is God when
   conflict wearies you? When others are too
   strong for you, what can you pray? See
   Psalm 142:6.
4. Do men and women handle conflict dif-
   ferently? Discuss.
5. Why does conflict sometimes turn into a
   power struggle? What can you do when
   this happens?
6. Read Proverbs 24:15-18. What does it
   mean to "lie in wait like an outlaw"?
   To "gloat when your enemy falls"?
   How do these descriptions apply to
   conflict?
7. How can you better surrender your conflicts to God?

LESSON TWO

1. Why should you persevere through conflict? List at least five benefits.
2. Let one group member pick an issue about which she has strong feelings. Ask the other members of the group to take an opposite view. After a five-minute discussion, ask her: How do you feel? How can you hold steady? Is it difficult? Explain.
3. Read Ephesians 6:10-18. Discuss each piece of the armor of God and how you can use it when faced with conflict.
4. Reread Ephesians 6:13. In conflict, what does it mean "to stand"?
5. At what point in conflict are you most tempted to run? Discuss ways to ride the rough waves.
6. What does running from conflict accomplish? Is running ever God's will for us in conflict? Explain.

LESSON THREE

1. In conflict, what is God's desire for His people according to 1 Peter 1:22? As a group, list ways you can love deeply while in conflict.
2. Study 2 Corinthians 2:5-8. How can you restore a relationship after being hurt in conflict?
3. Read Colossians 2:6-7, 3:15. How does thankfulness make room for the peace of Christ to rule in our hearts?

4. What qualities draw you into relationships with others? When conflict erupts and you recognize the absence of these qualities, can you choose to love anyway? Discuss.
5. If warned ahead of time that loving someone will involve pain, would you enter into the relationship? Why, or why not?
6. Does love ever require that you withdraw from a relationship? Discuss and give examples.

LESSON FOUR

1. What causes conflict to reach a stalemate? How do you feel when that happens?
2. Read Romans 14:13. In conflict, what does it mean to put an obstacle in someone's way?
3. Sometimes blocked conflict makes it difficult to function in other areas of life. How can you keep moving when conflict with another person stays unresolved?
4. What does it mean to "devote yourselves to prayer, being watchful and thankful" (Colossians 4:2)? How can you apply this verse to preventing or working through conflict?
5. What can you do when conflict is blocked because the other person will not take responsibility for it?
6. Sometimes you may be blocking the conflict. How can you stay open to the Holy

Spirit so He can reveal your part? Discuss practical ways.
7. Is there a time when you should walk away from blocked conflict?
8. How do you keep your heart from becoming bitter in conflict?

LESSON FIVE

1. What does it mean to bring closure to conflict? Discuss various ways this happens.
2. Why is it so important to bring closure to conflict?
3. How do you feel when you can't bring closure to conflict? Are you afraid of unresolved conflict?
4. Read Luke 9:5. In conflict, what do you think it means to "shake the dust off your feet"?
5. How can you know Christ better through conflicts with other people? See Philippians 3:10.
6. Are you feeling hopeless about bringing closure to a conflict? What can you do?
7. How do you bring closure to conflict when the opposing party has died? ∎

Gloria Chisholm is a single parent of five children and a freelance writer who has published three books and numerous articles in Christian magazines.

Gloria works as a full-time acquisitions editor for Aglow Publications and as a part-time fiction instructor for the Writer's Digest School. She lives in Lynnwood, Washington. ∎

Toward Productive Conflict

*Resources for further help
and study.*

Arterburn, Stephen F., and David A. Stoop, Ph.D. *When Someone You Love Is Someone You Hate*. Waco, TX: Word, 1988. Cassette tapes are available from Out Reach Ministries, (714) 494-8894.

Backus, William, Ph.D. *Telling Each Other the Truth*. Minneapolis, MN: Bethany, 1985. A tape is also available.

Davis, Ron Lee. *Healing Life's Hurts*. Waco, TX: Word, Inc., 1986.

Maloney, H. Newton. *When Getting Along Seems Impossible*. Old Tappan, NJ: Fleming H. Revell Co, 1989.

Phillips, Bob. *The Delicate Art of Dancing with Porcupines*. Ventura, CA: Regal Books, 1989.

Rush, Myron. *Hope for Hurting Relationships*. Wheaton, IL: Victor Books, 1989. ■

OTHER TITLES IN THIS SERIES

Additional *CRISISPOINTS* Bible studies
include:

> *Getting a Grip on Guilt* by Judith
> Couchman. Learn to live a life free
> from guilt.

> *Nobody's Perfect, So Why Do I Try to Be?*
> by Nancy Groom. Get over the need to do
> everything right.

> *So What If You've Failed?* by Penelope J.
> Stokes. Use your mistakes to become a
> more loving, godly woman.

> *When Your Marriage Disappoints You*
> by Janet Chester Bly. Hope and help for
> improving your marriage.

> *You're Better Than You Think!* by
> Madalene Harris. How to overcome
> shame and develop a healthy self-image.

These studies can be purchased at a
Christian bookstore. Or order a catalog from
NavPress, Customer Services, P. O. Box
6000, Colorado Springs, CO 80934. Or call
1-800-366-7788 for information. ■